BIG NOSE

Other Poetry by David R. Slavitt

BIG NOSE

POEMS BY **David R. Slavitt**

Louisiana State University Press

Baton Rouge and London

1983

Designer: Barbara Werden
Typeface: Linotron Melior
Typesetter: Graphic Composition, Inc.
Printer and binder: Thomson-Shore, Inc.

Grateful acknowledgment is made to the editors of the following publications, in which the poems listed originally appeared: *Poetry*, for "Last Days at Delphi" and "Museum Piece," copyright © 1982 by the Modern Poetry Association, and *Poultry: A Magazine of Voice*, for "Broads"; and to Palaemon Press, which published "Agamemnon Speaks" as a broadside.

Library of Congress Cataloging in Publication Data

Slavitt, David R., 1935–
Big nose.

I. Title.
PS3569.L3B5 1983   811'.54   82–21643
ISBN 0–8071–1072–8
ISBN 0–8071–1073–6

Publication of this book has been supported by a grant from the National Endowment for the Arts in Washington, D.C., a federal agency.

In memory of Adrien Stoutenburg

The epoch lingers and the dead stay dead,
though nothing in these latitudes can perish.
Decay is unknown, whether of flesh or language.
Hands that clasped once are forever clasped,
and love preserved is forever risen . . .

from Heroes, Advise Us

CONTENTS

I
Axioms and Assumptions

II
Imports and Domestics

III
Throwaways and Encores

I

Axioms and Assumptions

TO HIS READER

Let us cut the crap. This old pretense
of a common decency or culture or even
sense is a dead horse the stupid cop
dragged around the corner from Kosciusko
to Green which he could spell. Talk about stupid!
What else is there to talk about? The fine
modulation of a cadence? A pang
of remorse and a pain in the ass to the few of us still
able to pick it out. The rest don't
give a shit. Or shit all over it. You,
you son of a bitch! I'm talking to you. Listen.
You weren't my first choice but will have to do.
And don't try to wriggle out and join me,
turning tail, coat, and Quisling, leaving
them. Back! Down! What you lack in ardor
you make up by the smallness of your numbers.
Princes and counts, grandsons of thugs and thieves,
were a fine lot compared to you whose agents
are department chairmen, lecture committee members,
editors, hired readers, losers, careerist
louts, toadies, turds. A pure indifference
is easier to take than this corrupt
inattentive attention you dare deign.
The expense of spirit is this—for years we are told
how virtue will be rewarded, but find out
it isn't true. Hard to swallow. Harder
is how virtue is punished everywhere
and always: any man who's not too good
for the job he's doing, isn't good enough.
That's pain, maybe not dramatic
(Help this child to live? Or turn the page?)
but fundamental, fraying the social fabric
at the seat of its pants. In a random universe,
that much order is tantalizing, taunting.
Who wouldn't retreat to his library, shrink
the horizon to a golden lamplit circle

3

of which he's sovereign? Exiled, diminished, bitter,
bickering as émigrés are always,
we form committees to write our angry letters,
learning to doubt each other until we are sure
of the grounds for our detestations. You are untrue
to all that made us special, worse than the hordes
of dummies we have always hated and feared,
having treated them badly (as they deserved).
But you, with your good manners, your pretensions
to civility and taste—you're a disgrace.
Junkies, hitting gas stations, go to pounds
for bitches in heat to occupy the attack dogs.
I used to worry about them, the addict-thieves'
whore-dogs. What could be lower than that?
An assistant professor of English, screwed from his job
by his department chairman the arts and sciences
dean has buggered again. Editors, agents,
reviewers, book buyers, the Dalton chain,
Waldenbooks, the seven paperback czars,
all your creatures, surrogates, your thugs
doing your dirty work, pretending to culture
exactly as you pretend, which is pretty badly.
Thief or dog, which should I hate? You squirm
in your seats and try to join me again, to agree . . .
By what right? You and Helen Vendler
deserve each other. You and Harvey Shapiro
invent each other every week—correctly.
The sovereign is still accountable for something—
the table legs and chairs that bear his name,
straight or curved, plain or carved, Louis
Quatorze, Quinze, Seize . . . Demos, the one
and only, you are it, and responsible
for what you live with—this room and these chairs
first and maybe last of all. Grossfart,
King of the Visigoths, was finical
compared to you, chose which log to squat on
with a care and assurance you don't have. The poem
is dead. Its ghost is floating over the quad
when the moon's right. Its size and shape are the same,
but its weight is gone; it cannot carry the burden
it used to. You, the lovers of *gravitas*,
of empty ideas or fulsome descriptions of things—

4

furniture, fabrics, flatware, food, the dreary
novelist's flummery—you killed it. "I?"
says Turkey-lurkey. Right, turkey, you!
Its wraith, weightless, hovers where it walked,
trying to look the aristocrat gone some to seed,
but difficult to distinguish from the mad
unemployed who stare into crowds, asking
why you and not me? resisting
the feeling of taint. It is no accident
but part of the art, its heart, to make us misfits,
self-conscious, as only impostors are,
and hostile. Like love, it's a disease
with predictable symptoms, a chronic debility
that may remit in the early to middle twenties
but can, in certain stubborn cases, persist,
intermittent, annoying, something like herpes,
trivially shameful. There is no cure,
but all of us are mortal. Medicine's failure,
inevitable, universal, and fair,
allows the consideration of other questions:
how to behave in the tumbrel, how to defy
the mob's garlicky breath, its mean delight
in cruel amusements, how to struggle against
the terrible temptation to surrender,
join them, play to them, and hope they'll admit,
after the blade has stilled their hubbub, awe
or some lesser acknowledgment . . . Who cares
what they think? Who even thinks they think?
Like God they tease us to believe in them,
popping up, just like those shabby sunsets
that blew the romantics away, or mountains, or sea,
the Theological Outdoor Advertising
Company's banal dioramas. Bullshit!
Dignity, however threadbare, turns
away from such displays. Honest is better—
to swallow the bitter spoonful (Good boy! Big boy!
All gone). I know you well enough,
as the mind knows the body. They need each other,
despite their mutual treasons. Any idea,
noble or mean, mocks the flesh that bears
but cannot comprehend it. The mere meat
triumphs in the end. Even the glutton,

lecher, and sloth learn how it brings down
our temples of pretension. You and I
depend thus on one another, and serve,
but you are not my friend. Nor am I yours.

SPY

Operating behind the enemy lines,
I never know in advance what I'm looking for
or what details may be useful or show designs
of somebody's high command in a dirty war;

even when I'm sure of something, what's tough
is encrypting the message and getting it out. It's not
like school where we had to learn all that technical stuff.
Our ears are cocked for a knock, a shout, a shot.

One becomes accustomed, addicted to fear,
and the danger is what makes some of us go,
after the first time anyway. It's queer.
Habit, I should think. Or shame. We know

how HQ hates us, how we make them doubt
their pips and flashes as the mere children's games
all certainties are. They can't figure out
how to behave to people who use false names.

Despising and needing us, both, they grow to hate
what makes them so uneasy. And we can tell—
because it is our job to evaluate
just such moods—just how they feel: Swell.

We even tend to agree with them and wish
for such simplicities. A banner? Salute!
Sing the stirring anthem to purely fish—
or the hymn to the clearly fowl, which is also cute.

In a tall building with one of those grand foyers,
take an office done up with rich restraint.

Invite your prospects to luncheons. Throw soirées.
But as the angel passes, you hear a faint

dit-dah dah-dit from somebody's transmitter,
a comrade from the hostile zone whose report
comes from some hot attic or a cellar in bitter
cold. He's in danger. The message he sends is short,

but it blows your cover. Shocked, they take their leave
quickly, those new friends. And it's no surprise,
for intelligence questions everything they believe—
except that shooting may be too good for spies.

LAST DAYS AT DELPHI

We used to speak for the god, with the god's voice,
and kings came to offer us their treasures
for our inspired treasure, while the breathless
world listened for what we'd say. No more.

We have become a tourist attraction, pretending
for small donations . . . Oh, some old wives, provincial
and superstitious enough, still come,
believing a little. I think they are disappointed.
What can our hexameters mean to them?

The trouble is with ourselves no longer believing
(in spite of the world's indifference, the emperor's wrath).
Being illegal and going underground
can have—as the Christians ought to know—glamour.
I'd half hoped there might be a little revival
after Theodosius proscribed us.
It didn't help. One wonders why he bothered.

The Pythias speak, but only to one another.
Our white robes, our laurel leaves, our ablutions
in the fountain at Parnassus' foot, the stool,
the vapors from the cleft rock, the shivers . . .
We go through the forms, expecting nothing. The risk

is nothing. The emperor doesn't fear us.
But not to do these things would be rude, cruel,
would burden our burdened sisters with still more doubt.
Each of us has enough and has learned to bear it
each in her own way. Mine is to wonder
what other life I could make for myself, how else
to pass this month in the springtime, what possible use
to put this knack of making hexameter lines
as golden settings for paradoxical gems.

Besides, who can say, positively,
the god will not rouse? Apollo, nodding,
may yet wake, may wish to speak, to command
a new Croesus. How will the goats speak for him?

Nero plundered ten thousand talents here.
Shall I presume to rob Delphi of mine?

"Even if all of us here are frauds, I
am the best fraud." So each declares to herself.

THE BEGINNING

A wind at Aulis bellies the sails, confirming
the judgment of the crazy priest, Calchas,
as that of the god too: a breath for a breath.
It is no cruel lapse but the world's rule.
Men stowing their gear aboard cheer
King Agamemnon up on the bluff gazing
east as if he already sees a city
shimmer in heat and brimming tears, blazing.
Why bother to move? Iphegeneia's
cries will echo exactly in Trojan throats.
Not every ending is great with new beginnings,
but any beginning is a kind of death.
Obedient as a foot soldier to orders,
he blinks his vision back, descends, embarks.

EURYBATES

for Michael Palumbo

So the Aga sends Talthybios and me
down the strand to the barren sea and the tents
of the Myrmidons where the man is,
sulking. And we find him there; we look;
he looks. We just stand there, scared,
unable to move either foot or mouth, and gape.

The man looks at us and we know he knows
what we've come to say and to do, knows
what we would say if the spit weren't dry in our mouths,
our teeth, stones. And the man says, Hey,
it's okay, it's not your fault, don't sweat it.
And tells Patroklos to go and get the girl
and hand her over.
                    BUT
You two are witnesses, you two
see the insult. Let the Aga know
in his sick mind not to hallucinate
that when they need me and he needs me
I'll do another thing for them or him
                                    EVER.

And when Patroklos handed the unwilling
girl over, the man turned away,
walked down the beach a way, alone.
Talthybios and I could see him, hear him
weeping and praying. We took Briseïs away,
back with us, as we'd been ordered to do.

AGAMEMNON SPEAKS

B123–130

If we and they agreed, which is most unlikely,
but if. And we were then to divide ourselves
into groups of ten—to make the arithmetic easy.
Besides, eight is hard to seat. And six?
It's cheap; it looks cheap, the same way twelve

looks too formal, showy, and conversation
breaks up into groups. I've seen it happen.
So ten, then, and that's on our side. They,
and not all of them—only the householders—
come one at a time, as servants, footmen, or say
cupbearers, not that there's really a difference,
except that it sounds so primitive. Oriental!
As, technically, they are—oriental, I mean.
Anyway, if we wanted to do this, were willing
to go through with these strenuous arrangements
here, down on the beach, out in the sun,
or there, close to the walls, so that the cups
wouldn't have to be borne so far . . . I say,
at the right time of day, the walls' shadows
could make it fairly tolerable, the heat
being what it is here . . . It's a thought.
Under the walls then, the tens of us,
and for each ten Achaians, the one Trojan
servant. Well, you get my point? You see?

There really are more of us than there are of them.

PICASSO

1

Dora Maar said he had five needs:
a woman to love; a poet, his catalyst;
a place to live; his friends to encourage him;
and a dog. Talent? Talent he assumed.

2

The dog is an admission of the body,
a simpler keener self . . . if sentimental.
The alternative is a lack of feeling, thought
heartless and unbodied. One needs a dog.

3

The place where light grows out of the roof, trees
hang from the sky, and dark plays those games
it plays in bedrooms of good children, arranging
furniture, walls, guitars, fruit, faces
as if reshuffling decks of familiar cards
seeking their strangeness, one must own and own to.

4

A poet, of course . . . I should think that man
with no poet is no man, is less
than one of Max Jacob's baboons—or gorillas
to whom at the end he jeered, "I have your skin."
J'ai ta peau. He died a month later.

5

Dora's body, but Kazbek's muzzle and ears—
the face no man's, no woman's, no dog's land.
The paint on the canvas space was true to the space,
vertiginous and cold, the doctor treated
Dora for. All afghans are nervous—
sight hounds are. *L'époque Dora* ends;
l'époque Françoise begins: a new dog day.

6

A pipe, a hat, a certain brand of anis—
things as cheap or as dear as these claim
the rough terrain a little for those who know.
For the rest, the name flies through the windows, hawked
by vendors on 53rd Street and 54th.

MUSEUM PIECE

The signs are missing. Either one knows the names
of the streets or not. But the building numbers? Strangers
are not frequent here, *évidemment*.
Nevertheless, I find it, luck or instinct
having directed me right, the little museum
I've traveled so far to see and, thank God, open.

The exhibits, also, lack labels, numbers,
are oddly arranged . . . A hand-printed placard asserts,
"The objects on view are only a small fraction
of larger holdings; each is specially rare,
old or beautiful." But which are which?
Where are the guides or docents? Where are the guards?

Monsieur le directeur appears, abstracted,
but willing to answer a few questions. The guards?
An expensive pretension. Nobody comes to see;
why would they steal? The theme of the exhibit?
Significant Life Objects: A Retrospective.
Or *Instant Archeology.* Or *Junk.*

And the storerooms, he says, are full of it, and dark,
terrifying, and more than his job is worth
going down there again. The placard lies.
Still, having invested time and effort
getting here, I thank him and begin
browsing the curiosities on display,
unimpressive, pointless, until I catch on,
and then terrible—so that I feel naked.
Why is my life on display? That Indian hat
with colored feathers stuck in the corrugated
headband, wasn't it thrown away? The cases,
full of such trash, ridicule and indict

not only my unsuccess but my bad taste.
Magpies, packrats, are choosier. How could I live
with these things. The idea grows like a tumor
that my pretensions are not beyond question either:

if I preferred better, I had no right to.
These are what I was and am. This.

The conventional move here is to take it all
back, call it a dream, and let the sun
shine through a pane that is nevertheless cracked
and curtains that need washing. But love redeems—
or should—what habit can't quite blind me to,
and it's that love I invite or perhaps dare.

JACOB

When I was a boy, I considered it boyish,
heartily gruff, nearly stupid—goyish—
for Jacob to have wrestled with that stranger.
The style of it was wrong, lacking the danger
of cutlass or six-gun and therefore petty,
unedifying, merely schoolboy-sweaty,
without the suggestiveness of hide-and-seek . . .
Imagine little Marty Buber, weak
but wily, brow to a tree, his agile wit
considering whether he or God be It.
But wrestling? What on earth is a Jewish jock
doing near the ford of the Jabbock,
grappling, grunting, on the ground that way
with a sumo angel until break of day?
To that child's question, there is no reply;
the adult hardly thinks to wonder why
it could have puzzled, having spent long nights
in just such struggle and having learned those fights
are grubby, sweaty, and the muscles ache
from bruises only dirty fighters make.
Stiff in the morning, groggy from the bad
dreams that may have been wakeful thoughts I had
in the tangled night, I get up as sore
as if I had been held in a figure four
by some great goon—and think of Jacob who
struggled with guilt he should have been used to
from having cheated Esau whom again

he was to meet next morning. It was then,
you will recall, that famous match took place.
Coincidence? No, it was a classic case—
and the earliest reported, I expect—
of symbolic personification of affect.
But the label doesn't explain how, hour by hour,
the muscles tensed, the teeth ground, and the sour
sweat ran as he writhed in the tight embrace
of that thug angel breathing in his face
worthlessness and woe, regret, chagrin,
anomie, and the hopeless sense of sin
that lurks in all of us but works its worst
on the best of us. All night until the first
relenting in the east, he hung in there
in desperate struggle with his own despair
which knew and understood him at least as well
as he knew it. There was no fiend in hell
better informed about his wretched life
than this intimate stranger. Neither wife
had ever been so close, even in bed.
Its taunts all rang with truth. Discomfited,
he longed to yield: he felt his clumsy tongue
form the words in his mouth, but still he clung
a moment and then another moment longer
to silence and this stranger who was stronger
but with whom, for honor, he could still hold out
so many hard breaths more. And so the bout
continued—for the title, which he won.
Israel. *Who strives with God*. His son,
I can begin to guess what he went through,
take pride, and feel beholden as a Jew,
knowing that there's no help, that all alone
we wrestle with our angels on our own
at three in the morning. I have lain awake
uncertain whether my heart or dawn would break
first, and thought of Jacob, my forebear,
whose triumph doesn't help, although it's there,
a precedent, and has, I guess, its use.
The adversity of others can reduce

14

one's paranoia some. My father, his,
and so on back to Jacob, knowing how this
angel bullied, went down to the mat
bravely. What faith I have, I take from that.

II

Imports and Domestics

TEMPORARY RELIEF

By what imposture am I to beguile myself,
pick through decorum's crust to find that glade
or, better, grotto in which the raucous voices
of birds of astonishing primary plumage call
my half-formed thoughts in intimate excellent English?
Treasure is buried underground; the ore
never glints: think how under the blankets
that lode was formed from which we have scratched out
our netherworlds. To look at them too hard
risks Eurydice's life and our belief
in the whole flimsy business. We know how daylight
shrivels the lush dreamscape, that Dracula fears it—
a nearer relation than Orpheus and better
guide, intent on reviving first himself.
Each of us must learn and then relearn
the charms and spells that go stale like old aspirin.
We hunt fresh in the same dark where we found them,
where all dreams of light begin. The maps
of this strange terrain are more right than not;
but forgetting how we drew them drawing on instinct,
we trust to them too much and are undone
as surely as those who make their double lists,
advantages here and disadvantages there,
to calculate decisions and go broke slowly.
You see them, desperate men at the cheap wheels
of casinos in the afternoons, the servants
of their piles of chips and a system that has to work.
Outside, along the boardwalk, the tide is rushing
out or surging in, sweeping the sand
smooth and strewing gems for children to chase
and fools to ignore. Out beyond the horizon,
suppose a dolphin sounding the depths or leaping
into the light, its back a brighter glisten
for being wet, at ease in both elements:
such a system has to work—that poise,
the temporary relief that darkness and light

are for each other. The silence down there sings.
On the beach, exhausted, water still in my ears,
I've done that hop, hoping to clear them, to bridge
the great distance everyone seems. Nothing
will cure that ailment. I am a stranger
even to myself: with the unfamiliar
ill at ease; or bored, fidgety, restless
with what I know too well. But in that grotto
not quite submarine—there were birds, remember—
a place I had never been beckoned a self
I never knew before but felt fit
like the perfect shirt still crisp with its sizing.
A new shirt is a new start, a slight
change in our lives that may lead to other
more profound improvements. We feel that hope
more than we dare to think it and glance in the glass
to catch those first transformations. The voices
will speak to that handsome fellow or to themselves
(Dracula has no reflection at all)
so that I may, by cunning and stealth, outwit
and overhear them. Humiliating work,
like trying to outsmart a poodle, to get him
out from under the bed to take his pill
(try the jingling keys, the leash, the doorbell).
I am under the bed, the earth, the sea,
trying to trick that slightly better self
into speech. But shyer than any poodle,
I can pick up on the obvious dodges; shrewder,
I am sometimes able to keep ahead of myself
moments at a time. Go from a bright
into a dark place: your eyes, dazzled,
will see or seem to see starbursts, flashes,
whatever the jangled nerves of the retina mutter,
complain, or rejoice about in their excellent English.

SUNILAND

The water tastes peculiar now; the place
is foreign again and the vegetation strange.

The broad leaves of bushes are tongues speaking
in tongues that puzzled, tantalized old Adam
with near intelligibility. (What can
bushes say, for holy Moses' sake?)
I know only enough to recognize
a dialect I don't know. My parents,
when they wanted me not to understand, spoke Yiddish;
I overhear it everywhere now. The garden
discusses its place, its climate, the birds' and bugs'
acquired tastes with a single-minded calm
my arrival seems to have just interrupted. Poised
in effervescent silence, the tattered bananas
are merely dumb while I am stupid—they
know what my hair and fingernails know: to draw
a certain pattern from dirt, water, the sunlit
air, Miami's blowsy abundance, and green
into their placid being. Some blocks away,
in the yard of the house that used to be my house,
plants like these suffered my change of mind
when the new owners arrived, gunrunners, hitmen,
breeders of fighting cocks, counterfeiters, dopers,
who turned the automatic sprinklers off
and let nature take its course. The trees,
bushes, plants, succulents, pricey ferns
I'd put in thirsted, baked, not even cursing
them or me but chanting their ever fainter
mantras until they died behind the fence
those thugs put up to hide behind. Up north,
the massacres are as bloody and more frequent:
warm enough and long enough, a thaw
will lull forth February blossoms
tender as the gropings of adolescents
in the back seats of cars; a hard freeze
wipes most of them out. Only the hardiest
make it. And in the desert, after a freaky
rain, the crafty skinflint-codgery flora
open up to bloom like mad, to deck
the whole world pink, singing the hymns
we've never heard but Adam knew by heart
(All in plant-Yiddish? Oh, good Lord!).
That knack they know is the one I need—waiting
in rocky soil, rooted in patience and faith.

THE ELM

Late-leafing, as if shy,
it was pleased, nevertheless, to strike its best
pose against the western sky;
but that last elm is diseased, my children tell me,
and its branches die

as if touched in June, in May,
by a bite of killing frost from an autumn still
theoretical to summer people. They
can't understand it. I couldn't either, but
having gone away,

I've lost the feel of the year,
its times and seasons, jumbled them up, as that tree
has, so that quince will appear
to bloom with the hawthorn, the burning bush, and all
at once. It's queer

how nature contrives to mock
one's frailties. So Adam, hearing word
of the death of something he'd known in Eden—the roc,
dodo, or dinosaur—would feel . . . Sadness?
Triumph? Or shock?

Not having the right to grief
or ground for any other coherent feeling,
I can see each starving yellowed leaf
falling to leave a scar against the sunset,
like a cross for a thief.

AILANTHUS

The tree of heaven's a weed, grows like a weed,
its aspiration flimsy, its wood soft
for a wind of any strength to prune back hard.
In stands in vacant lots or along disused

tracks it flourishes, nourished on garbage, to rise,
shameless where decent trees would rather die.
So the poor, believing, crouch in their churches
as if to spring, in towns we don't slow down for,
their hopes lofty, fragile, and nourished on nothing
but need for a heaven they can't even imagine.
Hardier trees, oak, maple, beech,
live where the breezes of this world may play
their canticles of praise in sturdier branches.
Richly rooted, such old growth is earned,
but even the dimmest rays of otherness rouse
this rabble with so little to lose to dream
their jumbled jungles in which cartoon beasts
scratch magnificent hides on their majestic
trunks, or glades where jellybean-colored birds
cry in their moonlit branches. Rubbish produces
just such rubbish in a refinement
of justice either exquisite or cruel:
we frame our prayers however we can, and angels,
delighted or dismayed, answer Amen.
That tree, because it stands on the line between
our yard and that of our neighbor, survives. No one
yanked the knee-high weed or chest-high sapling
or hacked the man-high stripling down (or could we
each have supposed the other might like the tree?).
By such dumb luck—our oversight, indifference,
and misunderstanding—it survives, thrives.
House-high now, it would cost serious money
to take down, with that phone line passing through it
to make the job trickier and more costly.
The Chinese were the ones who called it the tree
of heaven. Every morning, in my study,
where my window overlooks it (and I try to),
it greets me with the day's first question: Why?
Such undeserved good fortune encourages all,
which ought to be heaven's purpose, to counterbalance
our lives here, refining this world's rough justice—
whether you stress the adjective or noun
(but that will depend upon your beliefs, condition,
and temperament). Your heaven and mine
will differ, but those malodorous little blossoms
must surprise us both who might have expected weeping

willows, say, angels could hang their harps on
sooner than this. There must be an explanation
homely and simple—perhaps that old soothsayers
and dowsers used the wood for divining rods;
or read the name the other way, as a warning—
an overgrown and overweening ailanthus
in the courtyard of one's house could bring bad luck,
risking heaven's attention. That information
(true, by the way) answers but cannot exhaust
the nagging question—how the junk tree presides
over my lawn, vista, house, and life
to earn its name, teasing with possible meaning.
Poets have taught us how to look at trees,
how to stare at their elegant leaves for lessons
worth our lives. But this? It is slapdash—
which requires a child's directness, an adult's poise
to learn how to live with and how to admire.
A sumac gone to glory, the tree is a crude
patching of earth and sky on a boundary line,
demanding more than it offers. Heaven, yes.

ACTS OF INCLUSION

for Michael Cooke

He gave up everything . . .
                              How purely crazy,
insanely pure it sounds: those lovers, athletes,
and assorted fanatics, their eyes narrowed, burn
and put us to shame who know that great giving up,
having often, briefly, been there ourselves—a novel,
poem, picture, or play can do the trick
so that we say: *This is the whole world.*
It doesn't include so much as make us forget
everything else, renounce for an easy splendid
instant what the widest sweep of an arm
may indicate to the horizon, even beyond.
(At Sotheby Parke-Bernet, the gesture is smaller,
more expensive, but still the same.) To focus
down to that pinprick of light that smolders, ignites,
and consumes is nothing. To keep the fire going

is harder. Hardest is keeping alive belief
that next time we may be carried past that point
of no return, contrive somehow to live there.
The passion never lasts for good and all.
The appetites and senses usher us back
to the kitchens, bathrooms, beds we'd nearly renounced.
A few of us grow finical (call it smart),
harder to fool or please (or call it depressed),
and trust to those common senses, the old retainers
whose too familiar remarks are at least familiar.
But even they betray and will usher us back,
holding out a juicy sensuous morsel
of affective detail to tempt us. The impulse to art?
Not again! The exquisite held breath
pains, bursts, and resumes its regular chore;
it leaves behind—appropriately—a fiction.

FAIRY TALE

And turned into a swan. The end, you thought,
because there weren't any more words on the page.
A warrant to suppose the uneventful
happily-ever-after? It's never that simple.
Yes, the swan was gorgeous, the kind of creature
you see once and dream of for years, a knockout—
the inelegant phrase nevertheless conveys
the sharp pain of perception there can be
at such beauty, that you and it can cross
paths. But after having spent all those years
believing she was a duckling and ugly, and having
been told by her classmates, teachers, and parents she'd never
do, she cannot believe herself in her own
transformation. Tell her the obvious truth
and all you get is a smile indulging your fondness
or else regret because it isn't so.
Some women were beautiful girls and know
their rights and powers as well as a major domo,
setting out the familiar guests' place cards;
but the fairy princess, transformed, surprised by a wand

and set down at the ball is not at ease.
Your duty is clear. You owe it to her,
to chivalry, and to yourself to make her believe
the story you must tell her, her own story,
how, once upon a time, there was a duckling . . .

HOUSE HUNTING

The primitive instincts whisper; our urbane
babble exhausts itself and the noise of traffic
remits for a time to let us hear their faint
promptings. Or, in a crisis, when the attention,
honed on stress, keens to their clear directives,
Fight, *Run*, or *Freeze* ring out like the gods'
commands the Greeks believed they were. Birds
of omen busy the skies, their maps and clocks
a wonder; fish in their schools maneuver, wheel,
put to shame the Oklahoma State
Precision Marching Band. The tiniest nerves
tingle, attuned to the theological swarms
of ant-hills and beehives, their certainties.

Dull as a bear in spring, I rub my eyes,
blink in the blaze of morning light, puzzled
whether to go ahead or left or right,
having no hunch to trust. Animals move—
animation being motion, the spirit's
choice of a path, a hunting ground, and a home,
its freedom and its nature. And ours. Ask
any prisoner, face pressed to the bars.
He has lost more than motion. Any journey
is one of the spirit, and where a pilgrim stops,
we mark the spot, make it a shrine, and summon
our scattered attention to how the hills are, what
the light is like, and what could have prompted the choice
of such a place to witness the passion he suffered
here. Our own should be as important, require
as much care in the siting. So, flawed gems
need cleverer settings.

We have been looking
at houses now for a month, walking the streets,
opening doors, and coming into rooms,
empty or littered with strangers' junk, trying
to find ourselves a place. The ghosts that haunt
Gothic towers or those of derelict mansions
have no such choices, inheriting their seats
like the first-born sons of noblemen. Our ghosts
peer from their dim recesses, trying to tell us
their lot—and the house on it—is up to us.
Gypsies, able to see their futures, flee them,
keep to their wagons, camp out in empty stores.
Less gifted, we close our eyes and ears,
try to take in a room or to sense how it
may take us in. Those instincts speak or don't,
and we bet our lives,
                        not that death is lurking,
quartering the same terrain we quarter
with predators' eyes. But happiness? I'll bet.

As does the spider who sends out once again
that first strand and spends the night again
hanging his intricate web, building his house.
His other choice is starving.
                        And the webs,
broken or abandoned, serve the needs
of other creatures. Men, for example, use them:
they're good for staunching the flow of blood from wounds.

IRIS

Bluer than purple, each as big as my hand,
irises bedeck our designer sheets
and beckon: we are given to understand
an invitation to lie down in flower-
beds, to quicken to hummingbird heartbeats,
or slow to such vegetative peace in our
repose as only formal floral expanses
offer to a bored spectator's glances

at such great swaths of color. The finicky ball
rises while the eyelid's languid fall
simulates a sunset streaming crimson
with the dark venous blood that vision swims in.
The lure is less of flowers then, than mind
calling to mind, a pattern set out, demanding
discernment and completion, understanding,
as in the dark when we are not quite blind
but can be confounded by our memories' tricks.
We get the room wrong and panic. Freeze.
Try to think! The opposite must please,
all those devices of horror but reversed.
The walls that turn elastic, the stolid bricks
ballooning grandly outward, the jewel, accursed
but shining all the brighter . . . Turn it around,
minus the minus, and then strew the ground
abundantly with these facsimiles
of flowers, emblems, nearly fleurs-de-lis.
Real flowers that grew in the dirt would rot,
cloy with the sweetness of death. And we are not
comfortable with what these irises mean
to convey, for they are Iris's, the queen
of heaven's messenger, whose secondary
office is the one we fear: she clips
the last wiry filaments that hold
souls of the dying to the nearly cold
bodies they can't quite quit unless she snips
them free. The association is very
easy to make of the mortal with the erotic.
The sex organs, nearly human, of plants
with which we make our beds are a semiotic
joke that does not lie, although we may
pull the sheets over our heads and hide.
The trite tergiversations of romance
by which Camille may cough her life away
conveniently to avoid becoming a bride,
matron, hausfrau, beldam, and then crone
make the connection. What's-his-name, alone,
can think of her always with that fresh frisson
untroubled by time's boring termite hours
that get to the rest of us sooner or later to gnaw
the huge supporting beams below our floors

until they sway: walking, we pitch, yaw,
and roll like foundering ships, like drunks. Flowers
don't disappoint us, but bloom like sopranos or whores
and die or disappear. These irises
emblazoned on our sheets proclaim what is
likely to happen in beds where love and death
rattle in our throats and catch our breath,
squeezing the light from the room to leave us blind
guesses, children's dreams, and children's fears
of an afterlife. When Iris shears that thread
and we soar away or plummet through the bed,
what on earth or not-on-earth will we find,
hurtled up or out all those light-years
away to a heaven where someone like Claude Rains,
impeccably tailored and condescending, explains
whatever it was we all along should have known?
The sheets we huddle under in the dark
are like those screens on which huge faces shone
in light that flickered through the celluloid
to burn into our souls its indelible mark:
images and moments we've enjoyed
enjoy us, turn on us, contrive to stake
their squatters' claims on lives we thought were ours
to do with as we would. These bluish flowers,
innocuous and terrible, preside
over our lives so. Only half awake,
I dream them on the hill above the spot
I'll probably be buried. Just a hill,
but from the flat uninteresting plot
my parents bought, the vision, restless, will
skitter about, then settle, satisfied
by the focus of irregularity
that gentle rise provides. Gently it looms
in many darknesses in many rooms,
a Mecca, a Jerusalem, to direct
even our faithlessness in the abject
posture of suppliants, our foreheads and more
touching the earth. What does the fakir see
who has stared at the sun to blindness if not this
glowing blackness in which a hillside is
another degree of black? The Arabs say
that the same blindness may come another way—

from staring into a woman's private part
which, of all the darknesses, is the heart.
Iris again, whose loins yawn like a grave
with a smell of flowers, faint and sour-sweet.
Dreaming of her, I wind myself in my sheet
as I shall one day be wound. To that small cave
from which we came, we will return at last,
unable to guess the future except as a past
somehow reversed, changed but familiar still.
Another cry like that original shrill
protest, and I shall see that darkness clear
to show me what I hope for now or fear
is beside the point—except for the subtle scent
of flowers, perhaps of irises, one hint
of what it would be like for me to be planted
like a bulb in the loamy earth, and then to sprout,
surprised, surprisingly gorgeous, and enchanted
by the spell that always lay within me. Out
of such apparently arbitrary connections
necessity reveals itself. Who meets
whom at the crossroad is fated, stage directions
having called for exactly this, forever.
The stupid never question it. We, clever,
may miss it: they are all designer sheets.

PLAYING BY EAR

for Joshua, off probation

Your fingers, puppies, scramble, fitful, pause
and resume their exploratory snuffle while you
appear, dozing but watchful, nearly indifferent
though somehow alert should anything happen to threaten,
too interesting, some novelty in the frets
to trap them as they cavort. You are not playing
music or even the guitar. Such formulations
are too purposive. "Just playing" is closer,
apparently frivolous: Platonic soup, waiting
for its idea to strike it, bubbles thus
in random rhythms and tones, suggestive of your
idle dabble. Tensions quiver, strings,

nerves, in patterns you may return to or not,
reorder, respond to, reconsider or not.
Let a fisherman stand in bone-numbing cold
casting his expensive gear, an idea
of hunger elusive as the trout he hopes
—in that sense—to play. Yes, your half-closed eyes
sharpen the ears that safecrackers rely on,
and financiers and poets, whose sense of balance
is there, the fine tuning, the personal hunch
nearly independent of data, assertive
of self. To be able to listen to other people
is the courtier's trick, the politician's knack;
to know how to listen in that near silence
to the nearly silent self is rare, takes courage,
steely nerves as fleeting moments die
one after another and you pluck new,
impromptu, out of nothing, not even trying
(especially not trying). The organized
lucidities your schoolmasters demand
may have some worth, but what is the point of performance
that risks no more than a memory lapse? Boring
machines are better than we can be at the deadly
fixities to which (*jeunesse oblige*)
you condescend. Do I have it right, how you sprawl,
unable to conceal from them or yourself
uneasiness with those so heartily cheerful
truths they're selling and you're supposed to be buying,
on that yellow couch in your room, an overhead light
playing on the varnish of your old Gibson
as you play on its strings, the sounds of nagging,
theirs, your mother's, and mine dwindling down
to subliminal buzz? Outside, bare trees
seem to have died but wait to come into leaf
with exactly the same leaves as the year before,
the year before that, and so on, while you imagine
tundra, jungle, gardens, whatever you like,
animating their branches with strange birds
of a plumage no one has ever seen and you
keep changing with each new sequence of chords,
harmonies for tunes not yet diminished
from their mathematical possibilities to mere
life in the audible world. To answer those songs,

bluejays, crows, and a few leftover grackles
trouble the icy air outside your dorm
with rasping moral tales about providing
for leaner seasons. Misers, vulnerable,
imagine thieves, reversals, watch their tickers—
stock or EKG—charting the tremors
that will sooner or later signal the almost longed-for
relief disaster brings in its hand like flowers
to a convalescent. You're already there
in that meadow, garden, hothouse, florist's shop—
it changes as you change your fingering
upon the guitar's neck, rearranging and sniffing
its delicate blossoms just at the moment of plucking.
Envy, meanwhile, grows like weeds. What dandy
indulges himself so in that earnest Spartan
training ground for Character? John-John
boozed it up, made out as they expected
(that is, without originality):
they fear flair or any subtler wealth
than they've imagined if only to resent.
Escape, for instance, that sheltered tropic isle
they disapprove of, you commute from breaking
all their regulations. My idea
of wickedness—or lassitude, the worst
of all its forms—was palm trees, hibiscus in flower
in February, the lazy leggy mincing
of egrets, white on all that vivid green,
and mangoes on the driveway. Pleasure, ease
had to be earned. You've learned better, or knew
from the start the pursuit of pleasure must be itself
pleasurable. It is no easy doctrine,
will not console you in difficult times, will turn
nasty, tell you pain must be your fault—
and you, I hope, will skitter away, suffer
foolishness no better then than now,
and hide in the instant as the feedback whines,
mirroring notes you've found from the amplifier,
responding as the world may do sometimes
when we have found the word or hit on the note
that resonates, being lucky, loud, and right.
They don't know how to do that. Neither do I.
You'll find your way, holding your guitar

loosely by the neck, letting it have
its head a little but still not losing yours.
A difficult posture. Have a good winter term.

VILLANELLE

My father's dreams unravel in my head.
Irrational, exhausted, fearing sleep,
I punish myself, thrashing a rumpled bed.

It is unfair. To him, too. How can the dead
harbor ambition still? Is there no escape?
My father's dreams unravel in my head.

His voice reverberates gravely. What I said
in answer fades away, is lost on the tape.
I punish myself, thrashing a rumpled bed,

grateful for his chiding. The tears I shed
are his, bequeathed to me, for me to weep.
My father's dreams unravel in my head,

and I am proud. Those dreams are what he bred
in me; they are the heritage I keep.
I punish myself, thrashing a rumpled bed.

He would forgive, commute, release, would spread
balm on these wounds, whose griefs are buried deep.
My father's dreams unravel in my head.
I punish myself, thrashing a rumpled bed.

MUSCAE VOLITANTES

The *muscae volitantes*, or flying flies,
do not exist, never, even in Rome,
existed, are like unicorns or the present

King of France philosophers love, as the new
grammarians like the King of France's hat.
Less rarified, these *muscae* deign to be seen,
float, hover, or dart across our fields
of vision, friends of our distraction, flaws,
impurities in the vitreous humor, specks
swimming across our specs, mocking our common
senses. Termites, nibbling posts and beams,
do less harm; these flies attack the foundations
of all our certainties. Believe your eyes?
Even the poor cave-pale and spongy-soft
brain knows better than to trust their jokes
and cheap tricks and learns to distrust its own
foibles as when angels flutter across
a roseate seventh heaven. Who has the heart
to blink them away like pools in the desert's baking
truth? A peripheral nerve in my left foot
has shut down for a week. It may come back,
but in the meantime mute meat thrives,
stoic, its present condition and future prospects
matters of indifference. The rubbery lip
and numb gum of the dentist's Novocain
are similarly brave. Should the nerve come back,
I'll be a tenderfoot again and watch
my step, picking my way through invisible dangers
and waving away these nonexistent flies
that cannot, until the final darkness, light.

OLD DOG

The idea of caves is a deep one: Plato's
hole in the ground, or Lascaux's, and bats, thousands,
their nervous zigzags signing the sunset. I
can thus construct a cave, except that they aren't
constructed, just happen in nature. Smarter,
I might be able to fool myself—or dumber,
I might be fooled. But that dog under the bed
has no metaphors. That cave he has found
is, as predators often are, and the fear,

the edge of which is dulled in us, in him
slices fine. The dog's odd, having learned—
from experience, that unimpeachable master
our elders always invoked—a fear of cellars,
a terror of being pulled from out of this cave
and put in another, less acceptable, larger,
colder cave. Five years ago? Or six?
Another wife, a light sleeper, objected
to how the dumb dog barked (not dumb enough)
whenever a car drove down our suburban street
or a leaf fell in a yard up the block, or the two
beans floating at random in his head's tar
touched. It woke her up. She gave me the choice—
put him down in the cellar or throw him out.
It was out of kindness, then, and out of love
for the stupid dog that I poked around with a broomstick
into that space he'd claimed underneath the bed
my daughter slept in, grabbed at the beast, tugged
night after night . . . How could I tell him that
or explain to him it wasn't an attack
or violation or betrayal? The dog
learned to fear how gentle can turn to vicious,
benign to abruptly malignant, and all cellars.
To this day, he won't go into a cellar
even to chase a cat, but will stand at the door
and stare down into the dark with a fear
I cannot calm. What he has learned, he's learned.
The choices deteriorated (as they do
often): "You can take the dog with you,
or I'll have him put down." And not to the cellar.
So here he is, unable to understand
his occasion for fear is gone. He just can't take it
in that he's safe, can't adapt to improvement.

Out of the cave, into the light, Plato's
creature blinks, dazzled, his eyes and brain
aching. But then he adjusts, swaps the shadows
for real things (whatever they are). The return
is hateful. He drags his heels. He kicks and screams.
But no matter. Plato's broomstick is long
and strong as mine. Back he goes. Down boy,
into the cave! But he doesn't get on well

with his fellow cavemen. Enlightened now, he preaches,
teaches, shows them their errors—and they kill him.
But that's too cheerful. The truth is gloomy as caves:
he didn't learn a thing, hated the light,
went back eagerly, missed the familiar shadows,
was welcomed home like a hero, having survived—
"How?" they ask. "I shut my eyes," he tells them.

The cozy cave the poodle cowers and growls in
is where he'll die. He's been abandoned there.
The demiurge has moved on to likelier creatures
and new occasions. The trick he's left to live on
is a bone gnawed bare. He worries it still.
It's not hard to see, in his red eyes,
frightened and angry, how old shadows dance
or hear in his inarticulate growl of challenge
Plato's answer. Afraid of light and dark,
of progress and retrogress, millennia later,
we have not yet found the good place—or we did
but couldn't adapt. His heart pounds. He shivers.
I hold him, stroking, soothing as well as I can.
My heart pounds too. We all shiver.

DOGGING IT

One of them mostly shepherd, the other a collie
perhaps purebred, both of them maybe abandoned—
or more likely jumped down from a pickup
back at the Maryland House on the median strip
of Interstate 95—they were doing a tired
dogtrot, the end of which focused clear
as my eyes became the dogs' eyes
watching their future unwind like a tape
on fast-forward: no break in the traffic
(on Good Friday?), no water, no way
to escape, even allowing the cunning of Lassie
and Rin-Tin-Tin together, no ghost of a hope
from the Joppa Road down to the Tydings Bridge
where grass gives way to concrete and the chances

dwindle even further. A happy ending?
Suppose the owner sees them, pulls off the highway,
whistles them back to the land of the living, and they
bound, tired but safe . . . No, it's Disney-
dumb, as I should like to be, to escape
the truth's sickening thud that all weekend long
happened or would happen or had happened.
Honest feeling razzed but could not rout
the funk that dogged my weekend visit. Men
were dying, and women and children, and great whales
and members of rare species. And I am mortal,
know it, and should be used to it. Those dogs,
being dogs and spared such foresight, worry
not at all but live in their black and white
certainties of the moment. Still the fear
suppressed here will manifest itself
there—I told myself. The bloodied meat
of roadside corpses (we saw one on Sunday
on the way back, north of the Washington Beltway
on 95) is sad but in proportion;
those others, alive but in danger, loping along
in desperate case together did me in
like that ambulance of the Animal Rescue League
that a week before had seemed to trail me around
as if it were an effect in some second-rate
script as bad as Disney's. Its halo of pained
yelps was bad enough the first time, but twice
more on the same day? Common sense rebels
and taste rejects such style of augury.
The shrill yapping faded—but sensitized
as to poison ivy or bee stings, I reacted
to those two silent hounds badly, blaming
their stupid careless master for my impending
sense of what must happen—and the dogs,
and the heavy weekend traffic. "'Cancel Easter,'
the Israelis wire the Pope. 'We've found the body.'"
It's an old joke. When the stone is rolled away,
as it always is, only the emptiness
is ours to face—or not—however we can.

POISONED WELL

Dying of thirst, a
man will drink from a well he
knows to be poisoned.

Demands of the brute
body suborn his thinking:
what can it matter,

quick or slow? Besides,
what was true may no longer
hold. How can he know

how old those skulls are,
grinning as if at a joke?
The well may have cleared!

Time, like the sun's blaze,
sharpens but then blurs vision:
he dips his hand in,

feels temptation, and
pleads with himself. He allows
just one little sip.

BIG NOSE

for Evan

1

The light bounced back a certain way from water
so that it sticks to surfaces as water,
and the trees all bent by the wind one way . . .
You recognize the set for your big scene
the lines for which you may not yet have learned
but the blocking is clear. You know you stand there, cross
to there, turn, and stand. The place speaks
as on a road at night for no reason,

38

a distant station caroms its long waves
off the ionosphere coming in clear,
C.B.C. Toronto or Fort Wayne
for fifteen minutes as if it were fifteen miles,
the genius of that stretch of meadow, that stand
of piney woods. And you listen to it. Equipment
improves, seems for a while receptive. The place
speaks, and to you, looking like anywhere else,
but different altogether, the air different.
A dog would cock his head, or sniff, or dig.
Men and women, having lost those knacks,
feel uneasy, look uncomfortable.
A frivolous thought—if I were a millionaire,
I'd buy it, just to have, just on a whim,
maybe to mark it for coming back to, later.
Silly, but that's an example. The fainter promptings
frivolity allows us to attend to,
birds bet their lives and species on.

2

Two roads diverge . . . If they didn't there wouldn't be two roads
      but only the one, as any greenhorn kid
can plainly see. Correctly, it's one road that diverges
      to make the two—as at Salt Lake City, the northern
fork going up through Wyoming and down to Cheyenne, the other
      running a little longer through Colorado
to Denver and up to where they meet again in Nebraska
      near Ogallala. We took the shorter road
(I've no idea which of them has more traffic—out there,
      it doesn't make a lot of difference). Rawlins
is on that northern road where 287 comes down
      from the Rattlesnake Range, Muddy Gap, and Lamont.
We'd done our miles and were tired, entitled to sleep, and Rawlins
      has a Best Western, a Holiday Inn, a Ramada . . .
The Ramada even has a Chinese restaurant
      run by someone who must have screwed up badly
the last place he worked so that the tong sent him
      here, close enough to the end of the line
to alert a reasonable man. It was the end once.
      That singular, slender, singularly slender
brochure they gave us back in Evanston with a fill-up,

the entire cultural history of Wyoming
in its few pages, told us the story of how the railroad
        ended in Rawlins once, till the line moved on
to make the next town the railhead. A brief boom
        like what they'd had in Laramie and Cheyenne
came with the rail crews, the gamblers, whores, thieves,
        and all that riffraff. Then they'd move on
and the town in a year or two would recuperate like a man
        over a fever, a little weak in the knees,
but happy he could walk at all. That was the prospect
        the sheriff of Rawlins faced and refused to accept,
considering it an affront to the town, the hills around it,
        his own honor, and that of the clear blue skies
you can still look up at and damn near drown in, gasping at thinness
        and purity and the clarity of stars.
I didn't see any deer, but grazing along 80,
        antelope, and there aren't a lot of songs
you can drive out to check out and report back,
        yessir, that's the way it is. Who knows
what quirk of arrogance or anal-compulsive behavior drove
        the sheriff to do what he did? It beats me!
He rounded up a posse, the way they do in the movies,
        Randolph Scott, and Gabby Hayes, and Yul
and Clint, and all the horses you can fit in a Panavision
        wide-angle lens and took out after
the worst of the bad-ass boys, the crème de la crème, the pits.
        The last shall be first, it is written, and first of all
was Big Nose George Parrott, he of the epithet
        Homer might have found odd, but this is Wyoming
where everything's got to be trucked expensively from the east
        so that anything home-grown, even a handle,
saves on horseflesh. Whether the malodorous reputation
        resulted entirely from Mr. Parrott's misdeeds
or was somewhat further wafted by the unforgettable name
        remains a question. My guess is the sheriff
braced a few of the barkeeps and the sons of habitués
        sober enough to talk. The pecking order
is clear enough in saloons—who gives way to whom.
        The point of it was exemplary, symbolic,
which gives our anonymous sheriff more than a touch of the poet
        or, anyway, ad man, which is a poet shrewder
than is good for him or us. The sons and daughters of Homer

aren't all as blind as the old man was.
Big Nose George Parrott. In the sheriff's random sample,
       in all of his opinion polls, that name
kept coming up. Knowing that crime is rather like art,
       and neither ought to be voted on by those
who lack the proper training, that franchise not extended
       yet (or likely to be), he was nevertheless
forced to the rough pragmatic frontiersman's approach
       and, like a Bollingen Jury or Pulitzer Prize
Committee bet on a name. They brought in Big Nose,
       tried him a little, found him guilty as hell
(of what, exactly, isn't remembered or written down
       in that brochure), and hanged him by the neck
—as judges say who dislike creative prison wardens
       trying to hang men by their ankles or nuts—
until dead. Yes. But they cut him down and then
       the sheriff came into his own, his scheme, his dream.
They flayed the poor bastard, peeled him like a potato,
       tanned the skin, and had the shoemaker (this
must have taken more than a little intimidation)
       turn the hide into a pair of boots
the sheriff could put in his window, a shopkeeper's display
       and warning. There was a little card to show
what the boots were, of what they had been made,
       and to warn the world not to try to follow
in Big Nose George Parrott's footsteps or fill his shoes.

3

Some scenes, abruptly lush,
command us or, melodramatic,
stun like Yosemite, while others
we choose for our quirky private reasons.
Still others choose us:
that hollow where she stopped, turned,
assented, or a similar glade
unremarkable, innocent
today, but yesterday alive
with the whine of bullets and men's cries
in the soft green of the undergrowth
as out near the Wolf Trapp festival
where it's hard imagining such discord

or closer to hand at Gettysburg
where National Park Service Rangers
seem to intrude with their uniforms
on a place otherwise so pacific
and delicate, you'd think that grass
was all that could have been mown down here.
So, in Rawlins, the rolling land,
the clean air, the intermittent
riffs of traffic rolling on 80
and fading away to let the crickets
vamp for a while lulls the spirit.
One cannot imagine anything cruel
or barbarous spoiling a place like this
even though, on the road from Munich
to Salzburg, Berchtesgaden
nestles in hills that are much like these.
It isn't nature that cannot encompass
savagery, but we, ourselves,
having our limits. After a point,
endorphins take the sting away.
My cat once flayed a baby rabbit.
I couldn't believe it was still alive,
that red meat, a butcher-shop
window display, but still breathing.
I took the cat away and fetched
a shovel to smash the rabbit's skull
and put it out of its misery
(and, I confess, me out of mine).
I realize now, it was long since
past that line, feeling nothing,
a beneficiary of nature's
grudging mercy. Big Nose George
couldn't have felt the rest of it either,
after the drop and ejaculation
hanged men are supposed to have.
The rest was the sheriff's grisly doing,
not to him but the general public's
pity and terror or just disgust
the manipulation of which he could
justify by pointing to
the prompt departure of maybe a dozen
troublemakers. Bad law

and bad art will turn official,
chew your ear off talking about
public safety and flashing their trick-
shop credentials: Junior G-Man,
Chicken Inspector, or Deputy Sheriff.
The set or the setting cannot save
the melodramatic historical farce,
even this. We left in the morning
and pushed on through to Omaha.
The skies were Hopkins-colored, the weather
threatened—a tornado watch
was in effect and all that day
a cloud's shadow followed the car.
Echo and Narcissus range
rough country where human voices
and human faces pop out of nowhere,
. your own or one that's close enough
to what you recognize or fear,
speaking to you on serious subjects.
We've made Big Nose George a joke,
tamed as much as we could with gallows
humor, but it's two years now
that he's been tagging along behind us,
the shadow of a cloud or one
of those cloud-shaped Wyoming hills.

4

The great question remains: how does the spirit
inhere in matter, or how can the inert stuff
come to order, quicken, think? To deny
the spirit in things is as savage as to affirm
too easily how each rock, brook,
hill, or grove of trees entertains a god.
One must see the difficulty to see
the wonder of difficulty overcome
as on a summer night when the heat lightning
flickers in the sky and energy leaps
not in mere daubs of paint on a ceiling
but real, in the real world we stumble through,
or in the spring when the wind comes up and the trees
ruffle themselves and dance, like druids, like girls,

welcoming the rain. Wind and water
and light riddle us down to little children
and up to awe. Say lightning hits a tree,
you go to look, don't you, to examine
what is special, holy, a place where it happened,
an inspirited place where the silence of the hills
stretches thin so you'd think in another minute
something will give way and groan aloud,
or the river below break into sad song.
After the bums' understandable rush
to other less inhospitable places
the sheriff was left behind with those terrible shoes
and troubled and troubling looks from his friends and neighbors
to whom he had become a stranger, a marvel
like a charred, a blasted tree. Something had seized him,
some fury or demon held him and put him down
to walk their streets again. And it felt funny.
You don't just walk around in holy places
but take your hat off or put it on,
or your shoes, as in a mosque . . . Those shoes disappeared
from the sheriff's window, having served his purpose
if not their own. People avoided his face,
looked down at the ground, their shoes, his shoes,
and more or less abruptly fled. He stood it
as long as he could, but weeks passed and months,
and people avoided him no less than before,
more openly if anything. He became
invisible and moved through the town like a ghost
in the company of a ghost. It wasn't fair—
what he'd done had only been for the town
(but not fair either). He stuck it out
a good while before he gave back his badge,
sold his place, packed up, and left one night,
those boots probably tucked away in the wagon
unless he'd tried to throw them away. Tried
and failed, that is, for they followed him. Big Nose
George followed along, up to Montana
and across the border into Saskatchewan
where he disappeared, looking for that holy
place to purge the holy taint he carried.
Spirit inheres, sure as hell, and tougher
to get out than dog urine stains

44

on your parlor carpet. And then the dog dies,
and you look at the place on the carpet and don't hate it,
treasure it, even. In Wyoming they tell the story,
print it up in a brochure and hand it out,
proud not so much of what happened in Rawlins
as they are that anything happened there and to them.
A twister touches down and it's terrible, brutal,
but afterwards people come to kick at the rubble,
sorry for the victims but awed and chastened
to stand at a holy place where earth and air
married to wake us from dreams of our poor devising
and remind us what they are and what we are.

III

Throwaways and Encores

AUBADE

First light, and birdsong grates
like the trolley wheels and bad springs
of actual traffic that swirls around them
scattering, as pigeons will
the smaller starlings, the real birds.

The change is almost seamless; pitch
and timbre, continuous, interweave
so one can hardly say at which moment
the old order of modest nature
has given way to the rude new.

NOCTURNE

The pillow's example teases: my heavy head
thrashes about with the day's rages until
I am recalled to the silence of feathers and down's
forgivingness. Such a simple lesson must be
reviewed each night and takes a whole lifetime
of diligent practice before one gets it right.

STOP

The trick of the *voix céleste* is that every note
has two pipes, one of them pitched sharp
to make that quaver and produce in us the effect
of effort, that tremolo of aspiration.
The stop is only half-true, but some lies
have uses, hearten. Who'd choose between false
hope and none. The organist up in the loft,

done with practice, puts on his street shoes
and leaves us alone beneath the imposing vaulting
in half-gloom, dense this time of day and year.

TITANIC

Who does not love the *Titanic*?
If they sold passage tomorrow for that same crossing,
who would not buy?

To go down . . . We all go down, mostly
alone. But with crowds of people, friends, servants,
well fed, with music, with lights! Ah!

And the world, shocked, mourns, as it ought to do
and almost never does. There will be the books and movies
to remind our grandchildren who we were
and how we died, and give them a good cry.

Not so bad, after all. The cold
water is anaesthetic and very quick.
The cries on all sides must be a comfort.

We all go: only a few, first-class.

TO THE EGRESS

1

The *grand jeté* requires energy
psychic as much as physical: that entrance,
so flamboyant in risk, must be just right.

2

Porch and vestibule allow
hesitations where the spirit may breathe
composing itself in the right pitch and tempo.

3

The tactful adjustment of light to adjusting eyes
and space to adjusting bodies: greetings, farewells,
ought to be gradual, like a slow drifting awake.

4

A window offers the landscape it has framed
that blinds and shades may blink away; a door,
one learns in the chilly hall, demands more.

5

A second story needs its stairway.
(Which was invented first?) In the same way,
a wall and a door inspire one another.

6

Inside the green room, nobody whistles, nobody
wishes anyone luck. The furniture' s scarred
from nervous plucking. Beyond is a door, and beyond
an arch that is like a door, like an abyss.

7

If glare affronts the pupil, the reflex squint
brings distant boughs into an instant's focus
prefiguring, mocking the deathbed vision—
or is it a mirage?—of understanding.

8

A downpour, too heavy to last. Along the block,
waiting for some respite or some increase
in courage and need, we are all poised on our porches
like fruit on a branch, and one by one drop off.

LACEWORK

1

Lace, yards, miles of it, bejeweled
to beggar popes and princes . . . Little girls
learn the craft in an orphanage near Venice,
make tablecloths and veils and underwear
discriminating—and wealthy—sinners adore.
Their elegant work is nothing to this
dumped free upon a deserted beach
by each wave . It tatters, disappears
as all goods do, scatter like faithless
infantry crying, "Flee! We are betrayed."
The early spring sunshine, nevertheless,
soothes: it's hard to care. Another rich
and doting wave soon heaves into view
to expire and bequeath another treasure.

2

So what? The wealth of the present? Nature's
glories again? Something like that. It fades
like the sea spume that did resemble lace,
shone with diamonds, seemed intricate. Was.
The sun beat down on my head; I was giddily wise,
supposing a creator who fooled around.
The self-destructive object instructs, defies
cupidity: Picasso used to draw
on the damp sand with a stick for the incoming tide
to wash away the hopes of would-be collectors.
Their rage, dismay, or grief, he found amusing.

The real lace buyers believe those girls
go blind by their mid-twenties. It isn't true.
But I know why they wish it to be the truth.

EDGES

Properly sharp, a knife-edge disappears.
You hold it to the sun to dare reflection
      but not even light,
        sliding, slicing, can dance upon
so fine a line or shine dull metal white.

So, at the beach, where a whole continent's bulk
hones down to a line a huge child drew
      with a thin stick,
        a pile of seaweed bandages the blue
and absorbs its ooze, just as the sea soothes thick

excrescences of earth. These edges are
tricky, where things are married that love to touch
      although they can never
        merge, and take diplomacy, some (much)
tact, and many excuses that may be clever

but aren't sincere: the danger is always there
of cuts so sharp, so neat that even time
      is trimmed a beat.
        Pain comes later, and then the line
reddens with blood from the hurt of the mere meat.

ZAP

Playing some TV game, the kids keep beady
eyes fixed on the screen where a random dot
of light will skitter across their killing field.
Their thumbs twitch on the triggers, ready, greedy

for the flash of death or accuracy—what-
ever you will, epiphanies revealed.

There are boring narrative lines on other channels,
but children don't believe in them any more—
character, plot. They have swirled down sci-fi funnels
to end up blips of light in this abstract war.
Now! And now! They speculate like traders
of presents rather than futures, having learned
what we'd as soon not speak of to primary graders
although on the tube, and their eyes and minds, it's burned.

BIRD

The flash of red turns out to be a bird,
a cardinal (in February?), turns out
to be an omen. Roman augurs knew
how heaven signs our fortunes and its whims
with the flights of birds; Noah with every creature
aboard trusted a bird's flight to bode
well or ill for the mood of a cranky God.
Crest proud, tail cranking, it lights,
letting me know in a cold time that grace
can still flow. And then she takes flight.
The dull red was female; her omen is clear—
for nestlings, fledglings, increase, a good year.

NIGHTSHIRT

Worn fabric rends at last: I blame
myself; I should have been careful, should have foreseen.
We know the fate of everything, but don't
know when the gavel will fall, or the ax, sooner
or later. It was an old nightshirt. Frost said
pajamas wouldn't last. He said, "I like
to knock my knees together, to know that I'm there."

The temptation is sentimental—what hooks
it hung on, what satin this flannel has rumpled,
what sweats has it soaked up? An easy emblem,
it falls apart as old cloth does, as if
history were good for something, as if
one's difficult hours or moments of transport
could brighten or tidy, silver cloth, dust cloths.

BROADS

1 *Diane*

If I were the kind of man I want
you to be, I'd be
beating the shit out of you
because I like toughs and
because I'm too sensitive/sensible
to put up with your double-
knit Orange County
leisure suits & your
hideous tan shoes.
But if you were the kind
of unkind man I want
you to be you'd
beat the shit out of me
or just beat it,
because of my stringy hair,
my tacky Goodwill/Illwill dress,
but most of all because of
my poems, poems like these
you'll never understand.

2 *Denise*

A dead bird
in a cage is not
depressing for I,
delicate, spooky
woman that I am,

can imagine songs
the bird ought to have sung,
had he been given
the gift—my gift.
I give it now,
transforming him perfectly.
I hope he knows now
why I had to wring
his inadequate neck.

3 Maxine

That everything moves its bowels and bleeds and then
dies and is buried or is eaten, or frequently both,
is pastoral and marvelous. O the country
is full of such wisdom: fields and stables are
abattoirs where the mallet of truth whomps
between my eyes. In the back of my pickup truck
is a dead horse, my birthday present, alive
with maggots and flies, busy as any city.
When I'm sad or out of sorts, I beat its bloat,
beat the dead horse, and the air hums, shines,
primitive, convincing, disgustingly real.

4 Adrienne

The griefs of women are quiet; rustle
like crinoline or whisper like
the tearing of old silk;

hum like appliances, give off the sharp sweet smell
of burnt-out motors; tap like typewriter keys.
The strengths of women are quiet
but hardy as the weed that finds its cranny
between the concrete block of the sidewalk
and the concrete slab of the wall, and grows there,
and blooms there.

Men are bums.
We're really better than they are.

SCHOLIUM

Palladas cites Odysseus: "Nothing is sweeter
than a man's homeland." And why did he think so?

Penelope, right? Wrong! "For in Circe's island
he had never tasted the cheesecake." Yes,

you can look it up (in Loeb, Vol. III,
p. 219, the last word on the page).

Either she didn't know he liked it or, worse,
did but what she made wasn't fit to eat.

And Palladas was correct, as Circe discovered:
there are limits, after a while, to the powers of nookie.

RAMON FERNANDEZ RECOLLECTS

for Robert Buttel

What he remembers is the portly yankee,
down for a good time, walking the beach
to clear his head from the drink or to get drunk
just on the salt air the way they can,
and a girl singing. He got very excited,
yammering on and on about the sea,
her song, Christ knows what. He wasn't rowdy
but pointed at the fishing boats and the sky
and talked and then fell silent. It was his tie,
the way he never unbuttoned his collar button
or loosened his tie. That's what made him crazy—
not enough blood gets to the brain. In Hartford,
are they all like that? It must be very odd.
Still, he paid in cash and he tipped well.

YO-YO

An egotistical Spaniard's perseveration,
or a Frenchman, recanting his too quickly given
oui, oui, the onomatopoetic slide
of vowels from the top of the palate to the throat's
depth figures the Yo-Yo's fall and rise,
the thing's indecent domestic question that small
boys cannot resist toying with: whether
what has been laid down will rise again
in the flesh, the spirit, or some unanticipated
mélange of these. The tricks, easily learned,
all extrude the suspense of animation
while the primary colors whirl at the end of their tether,
until with a finger-flick of godlike will
permission is given to rise again—and it does.

DISCLAIMER

A hand trails in the water shaping the stream's
bubbles of sensation, no mere babble
but discourse, a cool and lucid argument:
so a tongue in the wake of the lungs' plunging
scintillates with the baubles of sentience
about to break into fluent discursive phrases
any performance is bound to disappoint.